TEAM STEA

F-117

M000308910

specialtypress
PUBLISHERS AND WHOLESALERS, INC.

PHOTOS BY RANDY JOLLY

TEXT BY ROBERT SHELTON, JR.

37th Tactical Fighter Wing

**415th Tactical
Fighter
Squadron**

**416th Tactical
Fighter
Squadron**

**417th Tactical
Fighter
Squadron**

This book is dedicated to the thousands of people who have nurtured,
fostered, and guided the F-117A from a dream into reality.

*"To the demon that seeks the hood of the night, beware,
the one who rides the shadows sees, YOU!"*

Photographs copyright © 1993 by Randy Jolly
Text copyright © 1993 by R.C. Shelton, Jr.

ISBN 0-933424-45-0

All rights reserved. No part of this work may be reproduced or used in any form
by any means—graphic, electronic, or mechanical, including photocopying,
recording, taping, or any information storage and retrieval system—without
written permission of the publisher.

Printed in Hong Kong
93 94 95 96 97 5 4 3 2 1

Library of Congress Cataloging-in-Publication Data
available on request

Published by
Specialty Press Publishers and Wholesalers, Inc.
P.O. Box 338, 123 North Second Street
Stillwater, MN 55082 U.S.A.
From Minnesota and Canada 612-430-2210
Toll-free 800-888-9653

Specialty Press books are also available at discounts for quantities
for educational, fundraising, premium, or sales-promotion use.
For details contact the marketing department. Please write or call for our free
catalog of military history and aviation publications.

Introduction

Much has been written about the early days of the stealth program. How a few brilliant minds conceived their theories of low-observable designs and radar-absorbing materials. And how the United States Air Force—foreseeing the advantages of deploying fewer stealthy aircraft in place of vast armadas of conventional airplanes—set out to procure a revolutionary new aircraft.

The story of the design and birth of the world's first operational low-observable aircraft is a fascinating one, complete with strong personalities, government "hide-and-seek" methods for handling new systems, and countless dreams and unproven technologies.

As interesting and secretive as that story is, the purpose of *Team Stealth* is to relate in very human terms, with photographs and a chronology of actual events, how the dream became a reality through the sterling performance of the F-117A in the skies over Baghdad.

The F-117A and Operation *Desert Storm* were made for each other. Politically, the coalition forces were restricted to selected strategic targets in the initial hours of the war. The goal was to dismantle the Iraqi military without devastating the civilian population, and in order to strike fast and effectively Iraq's network of early-warning command, control, and communications capabilities had to be neutralized. The *Desert Storm* scenario was the perfect "proof of concept" for the F-117A.

Technology, however, can only go so far. For years the United States military has been committed to the theory, "Fight the way we train." Realistic scenarios such as *Red Flag* and *Top Gun* have prepared American and allied pilots for real-life situations.

Not only did the coalition forces in *Desert Storm* bring to the conflict incredible technological advantages (the F-117A, J-STARS, and numerous other systems and strategies), they also brought the best trained, most highly motivated, and skillful pilots and maintainers in the world.

Pilots repeatedly recounted how the difference between peacetime training and actual combat sorties was the visible anti-aircraft fire and the release and impact of live ordnance on targets. The disciplines, flight profiles, and coordinated attacks went "as planned" and were reminiscent of the training scenarios developed in peacetime.

The fact that Iraq's air force was virtually grounded from the opening phase of the war (and what aircraft were launched were quickly destroyed) is a tribute to the skill, preparation, and training of the coalition air forces.

The F-117A story is but a single episode in the war with Iraq. No doubt it is one of the most intriguing! For the first time in aviation history a stealth aircraft was operational in a sustained conflict in a formidable hostile environment, dropped thousands of pounds of ordnance with pinpoint accuracy, and received not so much as a scratch on a single aircraft.

The team members of Team Stealth include thousands of men and women in the aviation industry and their Air Force counterparts. Industry created technologies and

In the air the F-117A appears sleek, almost knife-like in profile. Viewed from the ground, the F-117A is deceptively large—65 feet 11 inches long, 43 feet 4 inches wide, and 12 feet 5 inches high—similar in size to the McDonnell Douglas F-15.

materials never before used with combat aircraft, while Air Force officers and enlisted personnel created a realistic and comprehensive organization and training program without precedence or blueprint—and, in the beginning, without any airplanes!

For most of the program's development, all operations were conducted at night in the remote expanses of the high desert near Las Vegas, Nevada. The program was so shrouded in secrecy even family members and co-workers were shielded from any knowledge of the "black" project.

The ultimate test of the program took place when the most visible and notable members of the team, the pilots, bravely flew an unproven theory into actual combat. The impressive results exceeded all expectations.

All the efforts to design an aircraft to evade radar detection and deliver laser-guided munitions with pinpoint accuracy paid off when the first bombs exploded in Baghdad.

10

The F-117A presents a different image from almost every angle. In profile the stealth fighter appears sleek and slender, while the view from above presents a myriad of angles and geometric patterns configured on an extreme delta design.

The success of the F-117A—as evidenced in the day-by-day chronicle of its efforts in *Desert Storm*—is a tribute to the men and women of Team Stealth. The photographs and remembrances which follow reflect the pride, dedication, and commitment exhibited by everyone involved with the F-117A.

The F-117A

People rarely anticipate all the possible consequences of their actions. Certainly Saddam Hussein never imagined that his invasion of Kuwait would bring fame to an aircraft and group of people that just a few years before were unknown—Team Stealth. This team—made up of contractors, maintainers, pilots, and the revolutionary F-117A—was born in the Lockheed "Skunk Works," raised in the high desert of Nevada, and came of age in the skies over Iraq. The first aircraft to strike during *Desert Storm*,

This view of the F-117A landing gear shows the heavy-duty tricycle configuration. All three gear assemblies retract forward.

the F-117A was also the only aircraft routinely targeted against Baghdad. This book is a record of that coming-of-age and is dedicated to the men and women of Team Stealth.

While the United States had been working on technology to hide aircraft from radar since the 1960s, it wasn't until 1979 that Lockheed built a proof-of-concept low-observable aircraft as part of the *Have Blue* program. This aircraft was a subscale version of what was to become the F-117A. It exhibited all the characteristics that would later be seen on its successor—a faceted design, radar-absorbing materials in the skin, and excellent stealth performance. Based on results of this program, the Air Force directed Lockheed to produce an operational stealth aircraft.

With development and then production of the F-117A begun, the Air Force was laying the foundation for stealth operations, and the 4450th Tactical Group was established on October 5, 1979. This unit was initially equipped with A-7D Corsairs. These were used for training while the 4450th waited for delivery of the first F-117A.

The rear view clearly shows the F-117A's "platypus" upturned exhaust arrangement resulting in reduced engine noise and, more important, a reduced infrared signature in flight.

The F-117A had its first flight on June 18, 1981, and the first production aircraft was delivered in 1982. This capped a development period of just 31 months—amazingly short by modern procurement standards. The 4450th retained their A-7s after delivery of their F-117As to provide supplementary flying time for unit pilots, as well as to provide "cover" for the unit. In addition, A-7s were used as chase aircraft. Since there are no two-seat F-117As, when a pilot is being trained to fly the stealth fighter the instructor has to fly in another aircraft, chasing the student in the F-117.

The 4450th declared initial operational capability in October 1983. At this time the unit was unique in that it reported directly to Tactical Air Command Headquarters. Another unique aspect of the 4450th was its basing. The unit was officially based at Nellis AFB, Las Vegas, NV; but all its F-117s were at Tonopah Test Range Airfield, northwest of Las Vegas, and all real flying operations took place there. Unit members, who lived at Nellis, would travel to Tonopah and spend a week flying and maintaining

**THIS PAGE AND
OPPOSITE PAGE:**
*Predawn maintenance activities
surrounding aircraft #813 at
Tonopah Test Range, Nevada.*

F-117As. They would not go back home until the following weekend. All flying was done at night, sometimes not finishing until near daybreak. Fatigue was an obvious by-product of this schedule and was a factor in two aircraft the unit lost in 1986 and 1987.

Despite the phenomenal security that surrounded the stealth program—the word "stealth" was prohibited from being used on any program documents—rumors began to leak out about the program's existence. Slowly the program was brought out of its highly classified, or "black," status. First, the 4450th was reassigned to report to the USAF Fighter Weapons Center at Nellis AFB. Then, the Air Force made public a photograph of the F-117 during a news conference in which they acknowledged the aircraft's existence for the first time. Finally, the 4450th Tactical Group was redesignated the 37th Tactical Fighter Wing, reporting to 12th Air Force, and the aircraft was shown publicly in 1990. At this time the unit's A-7s were replaced by AT-38B aircraft, providing a lower cost platform for training augmentation and chase duties. The 37th TFW received the last of 59 F-117As on July 12, 1990.

The forward-looking IR sensor is clearly visible just ahead of and below the windscreen. The downward-looking IR sensor is located on the right forward underside of the aircraft.

Following the Air Force's reorganization in October of 1991, the wing was redesignated the 37th Fighter Wing. On May 9, 1992, four F-117As arrived at Holloman Air Force Base, New Mexico, as part of the initial phase of the wing's move to Holloman, which will be complete by the end of 1992. At Holloman the new designation will be the 49th Fighter Wing.

Like many other weapons, the F-117A was developed in response to advances in an enemy's capabilities. But in this case the F-117A didn't just raise the ante, it made obsolete an entire class of weapons—radar-directed air defenses. These weapons had grown in density and lethality to the point where traditional responses—jamming and defense suppression—would have difficulty in countering them. The F-117A was designed to penetrate these defenses and destroy what they were protecting.

The F-117A is a single-seat attack aircraft powered by two General Electric F-404 engines. These are non-afterburning versions of the engines that power the F-18. The F-117A is a large aircraft measuring 65 feet 11 inches long, 43 feet 4 inches wide, and 12 feet 5 inches high. It carries all its weapons internally in two weapons bays. While qualified to carry most free-fall ordnance in the Air Force inventory, the F-117A is

Aircraft #828 of the 417th TFS shows to good advantage the dog-tooth edges of the canopy design to limit IR leakage from the cockpit area. Also visible is the port side intake screen and the uniquely angled forward portion of the aircraft.

usually armed with laser-guided bombs—in particular the 2000 lb GBU-10 and GBU-27, both of which can be guided by the F-117A's on-board laser designator. The stealth fighter has two infrared systems—one forward looking, the other downward looking—that "see" heat. These systems are excellent for use at night and employ an auto tracker that follows a target once a pilot locks the system on to it. Finally, a laser is fitted to "shoot" down the system's bore sight, thus putting laser energy in the center of the target. The laser-guided bomb then follows the reflected laser energy down to whatever the pilot has selected to track. It was this system that provided the fabulous video during *Desert Storm*.

The maintenance crew readies #813 of the 416th TFS for an early morning training mission at Tonopah Test Range, Nevada.

Key Personalities

It is estimated that approximately 45,000 people have been involved with the F-117A's research, design, and development since 1979. These 29,000 civilians and more than 15,000 military personnel combined their talents to make up the heart and soul of what has become known as "Team Stealth."

Ben Rich, known by many as the "father of the F-117," is now retired from the active operations of the famous Lockheed "Skunk Works." Rich was involved with some of the most revolutionary aircraft designs in aviation history, most notably the U-2, SR-71, and the F-117A.

Initially Lockheed was not invited to participate in the development of the stealth fighter. This was primarily because Lockheed had not actively designed any military fighter aircraft in recent years. Rich heard about the proposed stealth research and development through the Defense Advanced Research Agency (DARPA). "I told them I wanted to enter the competition. They agreed—and the rest is history."

Stealth research and development as we know it today began under a special program entitled "Project Harvey." Through Project Harvey, Lockheed eventually won out over the Northrop Corporation to further develop what is now known as the F-117A stealth fighter.

In the early stages of the competition, Lockheed officials built a couple of two-dimensional models to test their research theories. These models were called "Hopeless Diamonds" and eventually proved that Lockheed's research was on target and in keeping with the Department of Defense's requirements for a low-observable aircraft.

PREVIOUS PAGE AND THIS PAGE:
A pair of F-117As depart the EOR (end of runway) for the active runway at Tonopah Test Range, Nevada.

Lockheed built its two prototype aircraft as part of the *Have Blue* program. These two aircraft were built with $30 million—$10 million each from DARPA, Lockheed, and the Air Force.

Throughout the research and development phase, Rich and his design team maintained a confidence in the program that allowed them to voice guarantees to the Air Force. "We guaranteed to deliver an aircraft which would have stealth characteristics, be virtually undetectable by today's known radar technologies, and be able to deliver a weapons system with unprecedented accuracy. We've done that. Our accomplishments speak for themselves."

History will show that Col. Alton C. Whitley, Jr., was in the right place at the right time. The colonel, a 24-year Air Force veteran, was one of the original, hand-picked members for the new stealth unit, which began with approximately 10 officers, 12 enlisted personnel—and no airplane! In fact, Whitley was the first Tactical Air Command operational pilot to fly the F-117A. For this accomplishment, he received a plaque that simply noted: "In Recognition of a Significant Event, Oct. 15, 1982."

Whitley explained: "In the beginning, we literally made visits to the production plant and watched as technicians put our airplanes together. This was the first time I had ever been assigned to a unit which virtually had no aircraft. That soon changed

Though contacts with tankers in daylight are very much like that of other receivers, at night the F-117 is difficult to see until the last minute due to its black paint scheme. Many boom operators, even when expecting the arrival of the black jet, are surprised when the aircraft suddenly appears out of the night.

LEFT:
Aircraft #830 makes contact with a KC-135E of the 126th Air Refueling Wing of the Illinois Air National Guard. The 67° sweep of the F-117A is clearly visible. The swept wing design helps further diminish the aircraft's radar cross section.

when we received our A-7s, which we used as training aircraft until the F-117As came on line."

Whitley began his military career in 1968 when he was commissioned through the Reserve Officer's Training Corps program at Clemson University, SC. With more than 5,300 flying hours, Whitley flew 143 combat missions in the F-100, as well as 90 combat missions in the A-7 (as a search-and-rescue pilot) during Vietnam. He also flew 19 combat missions in the F-117A during *Desert Storm*. His awards and decorations include the Legion of Merit, the Distinguished Flying Cross with 4 oak leaf clusters, the Aerial Achievement Medal, and the Air Medal with 13 oak leaf clusters.

Whitley was initially assigned to the stealth unit from January 1981 until July 1985. During this assignment he served as a stealth pilot, a group staff officer, an operations officer, and a squadron commander. Prior to his return to the elite stealth outfit, the colonel was serving as director of fighter training and tactics at the Headquarters, Tactical Air Command, Langely AFB, VA.

Whitley was selected to return to the stealth unit as its commander just prior to Saddam Hussein's invasion of Kuwait. He, along with the rest of the world, watched with great interest as events unfolded and mentally prepared himself for a possible confrontation. He had no idea that he would be making a move from Langley to Nellis just in time to pack his bags for a history-making deployment to Saudi Arabia.

At 10 a.m. on August 17, 1990, Whitley assumed command of the 37th Tactical Fighter Wing. It was approximately four hours later that he received execution orders to convene his battle staff and prepare the wing for its deployment to Saudi Arabia. "I

LEFT:
As the wingman rides high and off the wing, an F-117A moves into position behind a KC-10A from March Air Force Base, CA. In this case, the KC-10 crew was from the 79th Air Refueling Squadron (AFRES). With in-flight refueling capabilities, the stealth fighter's range is limited only by the endurance of the pilot.

virtually left my wife, two children, two cats, and two vehicles packed full of household goods sitting in the driveway of our new home. I told my family I had to leave and that I would see them when I saw them again. I was very fortunate that they understood my responsibilities and supported me throughout the entire ordeal."

During Operations *Desert Shield* and *Desert Storm*, Whitley had several objectives in mind. Local training was required to orient the wing's pilots to the Middle Eastern terrain. The successful relocation and positive morale of deployed personnel were also essential for the wing's forthcoming mission. One additional challenge of the deployed commander was to get everyone under his command home safe and sound. The colonel accomplished all established objectives facing him. No F-117A resources were lost during the war, and all deployed personnel returned home to friends, relatives, and loved ones.

Desert Storm

During August 1990, the men and women of the 37th Tactical Fighter Wing began operations that would eventually cause many aviation enthusiasts to consider redefining the common military term—"air power."

Initially the 37th Tactical Fighter Wing deployed its 415th Tactical Fighter Squadron to Saudi Arabia in support of Operation *Desert Shield*. At the time, the wing's mission was to respond to Iraqi aggression into Kuwait and deter such action against adjacent Middle Eastern countries. The 37th Tactical Fighter Wing's commander later commented: "We didn't exactly know where we were going or what we'd find when we got there. But we went well trained, well equipped, and ready to execute our taskings as our senior leadership saw fit."

In December 1990, tensions built within the region and the 416th Tactical Fighter Squadron was sent to the wing's deployed site—King Khalid Air Base near Khamis Mushait, Saudi Arabia. In January 1991, a portion of the wing's 417th Tactical Fighter Squadron joined the already deployed forces. In total, 42 stealth fighters were sent to the Middle East to provide the U.S. Central Command officials with the precision firepower of the state-of-the-art F-117A.

37th Tactical Fighter Wing aircraft touch down at Khamis Mushait Air Base, Saudi Arabia—affectionately known as Tonopah East. Eventually 42 F-117As were deployed to Saudi and participated in Desert Storm: 20 aircraft from the 415th TFS and 22 from the 416th TFS. Although none of their aircraft were deployed, many 417th TFS pilots saw action during the war.

During the five months of Operation *Desert Shield*, the deployed members spent their time refining contingency operations. The training was so intense and detailed that the only difference between their training operations and their wartime tasking was the dropping of live ordnance. Whitley and his staff took the 37th TFW from stateside training scenarios to preparing for actual combat almost overnight. "We were fortunate enough to be in a location that offered us the opportunity to train extensively for our operations," stated the commander.

For many members of Team Stealth the war started long before the bombs were actually dropped. During the early evening hours prior to the first mission, maintenance and weapons crews diligently prepared the aircraft for battle. Capt. Sally Baker, a 415th Tactical Fighter Squadron maintenance officer, remembers: "Although we prepared each aircraft just as we had been doing for the past several weeks, we thought something was surely up when we made one simple change in our procedures. Because of an initial shortage of arming lanyards, we did not attach one of the lanyards on the bombs which were loaded on our alert aircraft. Therefore, when we were told

to attach this particular lanyard on the bombs we knew the bombs were headed on a one-way trip.

"I was shocked when it all kicked off. All I could think of initially was, Wow! . . . Then it simply became a matter of, We've got a job to do, so let's do it. I remember going around to my aircraft before the scheduled launches to make sure preparations were going well. I would ask each crew chief if they had carefully gone over their aircraft. Every one of them told me they had already been over the aircraft three or four times and were going over it again just before it launched."

Master Sergeant Sandy Herrington, a maintenance supervisor, remembers that "on the day the war started, many of our day-shift folks found it difficult to sleep. These folks didn't know exactly what was going on or what was going to happen. All they knew was that they wanted to be in on whatever was about to go down. As for the pilots, . . . some were nervous, some were outwardly confident, . . . but all were very professional and extremely focused.

"While the actual mission of the wing changed dramatically that night, the manner in which the wing's personnel performed the assigned tasks did not. We had been training for years in the hopes of showing off the F-117A's capabilities—and we did. We practiced and practiced and practiced our game plan until we had it down to a very fine art. We just didn't realize at the time that when the big game came along it would be the Superbowl for us. In my 18 years of military service, the 43-day war was by far the easiest time of my career as far as management of people and their duties. Everyone chipped in, pulled together, and did their jobs with very little, if any, supervision."

An F-117A delivered the first bomb of the air campaign at 2:51 a.m. (local time) on a critical Iraqi target just west of Baghdad. At 3 a.m. the first wave of stealth fighters struck their assigned military targets in and around central Baghdad to open the door for non-stealth assets.

As they returned from their initial combat missions, many of the pilots commented on the amount and the intensity of anti-aircraft artillery (AAA) and surface-to-air missile fire they encountered over Baghdad. "It was the damndest fireworks display I have ever seen," commented Lt. Col. Ralph Getchell as he was greeted by

37th TFW (P) photo

LOWER PHOTOS:
F-117As taxiing in to their assigned hardened shelter areas.

37th TFW (P) photo

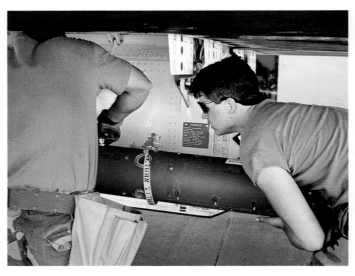

his crew chief. At the time Getchell was the 415th TFS commander and had just returned from his first 5 ½ -hour mission northward into Iraq.

As with many sorties during the war, particularly those involving F-117As, pilots encountered no anti-aircraft fire until their exploding bombs betrayed their presence.

Lt. Col. Greg Gonyea jokingly stated that Hussein and his forces were surely low on ammunition following his initial combat mission. "They've got to be out of bullets. I didn't think there were that many bullets in the whole world."

Of the 60-plus stealth pilots participating in Operation *Desert Storm*, only three had previous combat experience: Whitley, the wing commander; Col. Klause Klause, the deputy commander for operations; and one Operation *Just Cause* pilot. "All the training in the world could not prepare anyone for the emotions felt during that first night. I saw a lot of old boys become young men during the campaign's early days," stated Whitley.

Ordnance technicians assemble and load GBU-27 and GBU-10 laser-guided munitions. The weapons bay features dual hinged hydraulically actuated doors. Each of the two weapons are attached to a trapeze-like mechanism that retracts up into the body of the aircraft.

Capt. Robert (Rob) Donaldson said, "My first night of combat felt like it took a year off my life. I was the only allied aircraft over the skies of southern Iraq and Kuwait when I realized that every bullet and missile I saw was meant for me. Seeing those potentially life-ending factors brought forth many emotions—fear, terror, anger, hate. I never realized I could experience so many emotions at one time."

Lt. Col. Miles Pound, an operations officer with the 416th TFS, remarked, "During the wing's first attacks, some of us pilots who didn't fly on the first night were wide awake and hoping for the best for our fellow pilots and friends. I recall sitting around with a bunch of guys watching CNN as Peter Arnett filed his reports live from Baghdad. Of course we knew what was about to happen, and as our assigned time-on-targets (TOT) neared . . . we all anxiously glanced at our watches. We were so sure that our plans would work. So, as our TOTs neared, we did a countdown as if we were flying the missions ourselves. As the TOTs neared we said to ourselves that he (Arnett) should be going off the air right . . . about . . . NOW! And he did!"

Pound, perhaps like all of the coalition aircrews involved in the war effort, was greatly affected by the brief, but deadly conflict. "When you look at the desecration of Kuwait, all the people killed or injured, and to have people shooting at and trying to kill you—it all affects you tremendously. The perception of the tracers and anti-aircraft fire viewed on television by the folks at home was like looking through a soda straw. You saw only a small amount of the airspace. What one saw in reality, over the target, was the entire sky lit up. Many of our pilots said the triple-A was like the biggest fireworks display they had ever seen. They also said it was mesmerizing. For as deadly as it was, it was also beautiful: all the different colors crisscrossing the sky all around you." To minimize the beautiful—yet deadly—distraction, Pound would lower his seat as far as it would go until he had finished his mission at hand. "That way I wouldn't see the sky until after I had hit my target."

Pound went to Saudi Arabia as part of a third wave of stealth pilots to join the coalition forces. Following his arrival in Saudi, Pound flew two orientation flights with his third flight being a combat mission on his third day in the country.

A Silver Star was awarded to F-117A pilot Capt. Marcel E. Kerdavid, Jr. He was awarded his medal for gallantry and superb airmanship during his initial January 17 mission over Baghdad. During the mission, Kerdavid faced extremely heavy enemy air defenses as the first F-117As entered Baghdad's airspace.

According to U.S. Central Command Air Force officials, Kerdavid's determination to get the job done right the first time "resulted in direct hits on the Karkh Communications Tower and the National Command alternate bunker at North Taji." The award's accompanying citation further noted that "his attacks on these key command, control, and communications facilities helped pave the way for subsequent attacks by coalition forces and directly contributed to the historic success of Desert Storm."

Kerdavid later commented, "Awards were the furthest thing from my thoughts as I entered Baghdad. I just wanted to get to my targets on time and have two successful drops. The war's initial phase was a total team effort. A lot of things were happening all at once, and the success of the operation hinged on everyone being where they were supposed to be at a precise time. It was a group effort to do a good job that first night.

37th TFW (P) photo

A 2000 lb GBU-27 laser-guided bomb is being loaded into #813, "The Toxic Avenger," Colonel Whitley's aircraft.

Even though I felt very well prepared with my training, I was somewhat apprehensive about the aircraft. Its stealthiness had not been tested in combat, and everyone wondered whether or not this stealth stuff really worked. Well, we all now know stealth does work, and we did what we were assigned to do. We crossed the border to take out the Iraqi communications. When the tower was knocked out, it enabled our other aircraft to enter Iraq on their way to their assigned targets."

During the war, mission planners targeted the F-117A against critical strategic Iraqi command and control installations. Other vital targets assigned to the 37th TFW(P) included key communications centers; research, development, production, and storage facilities for nuclear and chemical weapons; and a variety of other targets—especially hardened aircraft shelters at numerous Iraqi airfields.

In preparation for the ground war, theater planners also tasked stealth fighter pilots against critical Iraqi resupply lines, including key bridges, railroad choke points, and major highways. Just prior to the ground offensive, F-117As successfully destroyed a complex of pumping stations, as well as distribution networks designed to feed oil into anti-personnel fire trenches.

As a coalition workhorse, the F-117A logged nearly 1,300 combat sorties while flying 6,905 combat flying hours. During their missions, the F-117A pilots delivered over 2,000 tons of precision-guided ordnance with a hit rate of better than 80 percent.

37th TFW (P) photo

37th TFW (P) photo

Although the 37th Tactical Fighter Wing Provisional and its 42 stealth fighters represented just 2 1/2 percent of all allied fighter and attack aircraft in the Gulf, the F-117As were assigned against more than 31 percent of the strategic Iraqi military targets attacked during the first 24 hours of the air campaign. The wing's workhorse attitude persisted throughout the air campaign as the F-117As attacked more than 40 percent of the strategic military targets targeted by the entire coalition forces.

It is especially noteworthy that the world's only operational stealth fighter was the only aircraft to be routinely assigned against military targets within the city limits of Baghdad! Not one F-117A received so much as a scratch from the formidable Iraqi air defenses. Such effectiveness, success, and survivability are unprecedented in the history of aerial warfare.

Black Magic
#789
31 combat missions

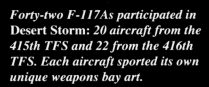

Forty-two F-117As participated in Desert Storm: 20 aircraft from the 415th TFS and 22 from the 416th TFS. Each aircraft sported its own unique weapons bay art.

Deadly Jester
#790
30 combat missions

Lazy Ace
#791
33 combat missions

Wiley E. Coyote's
Tritonal Express
#793
33 combat missions

Delta Dawn
#794
35 combat missions

Fatal Attraction
#796
29 combat missions

Aces and Eights
#798
34 combat missions

Perpetrator
#801
38 combat missions

415th Tactical Fighter Squadron

Something Wicked
#806
39 combat missions

The Chickenhawk
#807
14 combat missions

Thor
#808
37 combat missions

Double Down
#811
33 combat missions

No Name (Axel)
#812
42 combat missions

Lone Wolf
#816
39 combat missions

The Overachiever
#818
38 combat missions

Sneak Attack
#821
32 combat missions

Mad-Max
#825
33 combat missions

Nachtfalke
#826
29 combat missions

Affectionately Christine
#843
33 combat missions

**415th Tactical
Fighter
Squadron**

War Pig
#786
24 combat missions

Spell Bound
#797
8 combat missions

Midnight Rider
#799
21 combat missions

Black Magic (Witch)
#802
19 combat missions

Unexpected Guest
#803
33 combat missions

Dark Angel
#810
26 combat missions

The Toxic Avenger
#813
35 combat missions

Final Verdict
#814
34 combat missions

Shaba
#817
18 combat missions

416th Tactical Fighter Squadron

Raven Beauty
#819
30 combat missions

Avenging Angel
#829
23 combat missions

Black Assassin
#830
31 combat missions

Once Bitten
#832
30 combat missions

Black Devil
#833
30 combat missions

Necromancer
#834
34 combat missions

The Dragon
#835
26 combat missions

Christine
#836
39 combat missions

Habu II
#837
31 combat missions

Magic Hammer
#838
36 combat missions

Black Widow
#840
32 combat missions

**416th Tactical
Fighter
Squadron**

Mystic Warrior
#841
18 combat missions

It's Hammertime
#842
33 combat missions

OPPOSITE PAGE:
*F-117As taxi to hardened shelters
at Khamis Mushait Air Base,
Saudi Arabia.*

BELOW:
*Battle-tested F-117As await their
pilots and the cover of darkness to
continue the war against Iraq.*

Chronology

Following its deployment to Saudi Arabia, the deployed stealth wing was designated the 37th Tactical Fighter Wing Provisional—37th TFW(P). The following day-by-day chronology of the 37th TFW(P)'s missions during *Desert Storm* was compiled by the wing's historian.

While reading this chronology, one must keep in mind the unique mission of the world's only operational stealth unit—to attack high-value targets in a dense threat environment during the dark of night. Therefore, some combat missions were completed during the late evening hours of one day while other missions were tasked in the early morning hours on the following day—two separate days in terms of calendar days, but within one shroud of darkness.

As an example, on Day 3 of the air campaign, two waves of stealth fighters attacked their assigned targets, the first wave just after dark and prior to midnight on January 18, and the second wave after midnight on January 19. Both waves were conducted under one shroud of darkness, but actually on two different dates when considering calendar days. Unless otherwise noted, all time references are to local time in the arena of operation.

January 17, 1991   Day 1, Wave One
At 12:22 a.m., the 415th TFS launched F-117As against a combined integrated operations center/ground control intercept site at Nukhayb, two air defense control sector headquarters, and the Iraqi Air Force Headquarters in Baghdad, as well as numerous other targets that included radar facilities, telephone centers in Baghdad, and other targets of high priority.

Day 1, Wave Two
Twelve F-117As repeated strikes on the Iraqi Air Force Headquarters, air defense sector headquarters, and telephone exchanges in Baghdad; the Al Taqaddum integrated operations center/ground control intercept facility; military related facilities at North Taji; and the Presidential grounds at Abu Ghurayb. New targets included troposcatter stations, television transmitter stations, international radio transmitters, Rasheed Airfield, and communications satellite terminals.

Day 1, Wave Three
A third wave of eight F-117As attacked sector operations centers, more headquarters buildings, ammunition stores, and a chemical/biological facility. The "Voice of America" reported anti-aircraft fire and bombs exploding in Baghdad at 3 a.m. following the first weapons drop on the Iraqi capital by 37th TFW(P) aircraft.
At 8 a.m. (Pacific Time), eight more F-117As left Nevada for Saudi Arabia by way of Langley AFB. These aircraft were slated as attrition reserves.

January 18   Day 2, Wave One
Twelve 415th TFS jets were launched against Iraqi targets in Baghdad and other centers. Due to an air abort (the aircraft in question returning safely to base), only 11 aircraft completed successful runs against radio transmitters, command and control bunkers, the intelligence service headquarters, the Iraqi airborne warning and control system (AWACS), integrated operations centers, sector headquarters, and the national computer center.

Day 2, Wave Two
Twelve 416th TFS jets attacked integrated operations centers, headquarters buildings, communications sites, a nuclear reactor, and ammunition bunkers. Baghdad was hit again, as were a number of other high-priority locations.

Day 3, Wave One
The 415th TFS attacked communications sites, integrated operations centers, a nuclear reactor, sector headquarters, the Ministry of Culture and Information, Hawk

37th TFW (P) photo

missile sites and training centers, and the Ministry of Defense. Pilots encountered bad weather, which hampered weapons deliveries.

January 19   Day 3, Wave Two

Ten 416th TFS aircraft attacked various targets, including Scud missile sites; signals intelligence facilities; a highway bridge; and command, control, and communications facilities. The weather was so poor most pilots attempted to drop both bombs on alternate targets.

Day 4, Wave One

415th TFS pilots attacked bridges, command and control bunkers, integrated operations centers/ground control intercept sites, sector headquarters, sector operations centers, radio transmitter stations, ammunition storage dumps, and two telephone exchanges. Weather was once again a factor and limited success.

January 20   Day 4, Wave Two

Nine F-117As of the 416th TFS attacked a target list comparable to the previous three nights. Good weather permitted a much higher degree of success: 10 hits. This wave concentrated on targets in and around Baghdad; Scud sector operations centers, chemical and biological warfare centers, ammunition storage dumps, a signals intelligence station, military related facilities, bridges, command and control bunkers, and an integrated operations center.

January 21   Day 5, Wave One

Ten 415th TFS jets attacked a biological warfare facility, a troposcatter station, radar and satellite ground stations, a Baghdad television transmitter/radio relay terminal, and the headquarters for the Ministry of Defense and Iraqi Air Force in Baghdad.

Day 5, Wave Two
The 416th TFS flew 13 sorties. In spite of poor weather, targets hit included ammunition dumps, surface-to-air missile sites, Scud missile bunkers, a combined integrated operations troposcatter station, and a Scud and Frog missile site.

Day 6, Wave One
Fourteen 415th TFS jets attacked a radio relay terminal, Iraqi Air Force Headquarters, the main signals intelligence station, the international radio communications transmitter-receiver, two telephone exchanges, and the nuclear research center in Baghdad. Squadron pilots registered 20 bomb hits.

January 22   **Day 6, Wave Two**
The 416th TFS sent a wave of 14 F-117As to bomb Iraqi targets at Baghdad and surrounding areas, targeting surface-to-air missile sites; Internal Security, Ministry of Defense, Intelligence Service, and the Air Force headquarters, along with numerous other high-priority targets. Twenty-six hits marked the 37th's best performance of the air war thus far!

Day 7, Wave One
Fourteen 415th TFS aircraft attacked the Balad Southeast Airfield, where 21 bomb hits were recorded.

January 23   **Day 7, Wave Two**
Ten 416th TFS jets took off on time at midnight to bomb missile handling facilities, the main signals intelligence station, and transportation facilities in Baghdad; highway bridges over the Euphrates River at Nasiriyah and As Samawah and a highway bridge at Al Quranah. Pilots recorded 16 bomb hits.

January 23   **Day 8, Wave One**
The 415th TFS launched 13 of 14 scheduled jets against road bridges in Iraq; however, bad weather limited the pilots to only three bomb drops.

January 24   **Day 8, Wave Two**
The 416th TFS launched 14 sorties against bridges, communication centers, and an airfield, scoring 11 direct hits.

37th TFW (P) photo

37th TFW (P) photo

37th TFW (P) photo

66

37th TFW (P) photo

Col. Alton C. Whitley, Jr., commander of the 37th TFW(P), assumed command of the wing shortly before **Desert Storm** *and flew 19 combat missions.*

37th TFW (P) photo

Colonel Whitley is greeted by members of Team Stealth upon his arrival at Khamis Mushait Air Base, Saudi Arabia.

OPPOSITE PAGE ABOVE:
An M-60 armed HUMM-V guards the perimeter.

Maintenance crews ready four F-117As for twilight sorties.

LEFT:
A fully loaded #821 "Sneak Attack" of the 415th TFS awaits its pilot prior to a mission over Iraq.

Day 9, Wave One

CENTAF (Headquarters Central Command Air Forces) tasked the 37th TFW(P) to resume flying three waves of F-117As against military targets. For the first wave, the 416th sent 14 aircraft against airfields at Qayyarah West, Al Assad, and Kirkuk. One aircraft aborted after takeoff (returning safely to base). The remaining 13 jets scored 20 hits.

Day 9, Wave Two

The 416th TFS launched the day's second wave against highway bridges.

January 25   **Day 9, Wave Three**

Seven 415th TFS and three 416th TFS jets concentrated on enemy airfields, but bad weather hindered the effort.

Day 10, Wave One

The 415th TFS and 416th TFS each sent three F-117As after several bridges and an airfield at Tallil. Six more F-117As flew from Langley to King Khalid Air Base. These aircraft were assigned to the 416th TFS.

Day 10, Wave Two

Four 415th TFS jets took off at 10 p.m., and at 11 p.m. four additional jets were launched. All eight jets attacked Iraq's H-2 and H-3 airfields. Post-strike assessment indicated eight hits.

January 26   ### Day 10, Wave Three

For this wave, the 416th TFS sent eight aircraft to bomb the H-3 airfields.

Day 11, Wave One

Ten F-117As attacked Iraqi airfields, ammunition depots, and a joint integrated operations center/ground intercept site.

Day 11, Wave Two

Thirteen aircraft (eight 415th TFS and five 416th TFS) attacked Iraqi airfields, an integrated operations center/ground control intercept site, and an air defense control sector facility. The Qayyarah West Airfield was shrouded in bad weather, but the alternate target at Al Assad bore the brunt of seven direct hits. Kirkuk Airfield received eight bomb strikes. Another airfield took three direct hits, while the Kirkuk ground control site and sector headquarters were also rocked by direct hits.

Nighttime! The environment for which the F-117A was designed and the arena in which it fought during **Desert Storm.**

37th TFW (P) photo

With a Saudi F-15 in the foreground, an F-117A returns from a predawn strike.

37th TFW (P) photo

January 27   Day 11, Wave Three

The 37th TFW(P) dedicated a third wave to the destruction of Iraq's H-2 airfield and various Scud missile sites. Six 416th TFS and four 415th TFS aircraft took part in the attacks, scoring nine hits.

Day 12, Wave One

Three waves of aircraft were sent to strike airfields, shelters, ammunition dumps, and other miscellaneous targets in Iraq. In the first wave, 10 jets were dispatched to attack airfields at Balad and Rasheed, as well as communications facilities in Baghdad, including the Iraqi Intelligence Service Headquarters.

Day 12, Wave Two

The second wave (six from the 415th TFS and eight from the 416th TFS) achieved great success bombing airfields; a chemical/biological warfare research, production, and storage facility; highway bridges; and the Baghdad Nuclear Research Center. Twenty-four bombs found their targets.

Colonel Whitley makes a final check on a GBU-27 laser-guided bomb prior to a combat sortie.

37th TFW (P) photo

"The Toxic Avenger," aircraft #813 of the 416th TFS, taxis out to its 23rd combat sortie.

37th TFW (P) photo

January 28   **Day 12, Wave Three**

Ten F-117As raided Iraqi airfields, ammunition dumps, and a missile site. Six 415th TFS jets concentrated on the ammunition storage facilities, as well as H-3 airfield shelters and a surface-to-air missile site. Four pilots of the 416th TFS spent their bombs exclusively on targets at Iraq's H-2 and H-3 airfields. Sixteen hits were recorded.

Day 13, Wave One

The 415th TFS and the 416th TFS contributed four and six aircraft respectively, attacking various missile and communications sites in and around Baghdad. Fifteen targets were hit.

Day 13, Wave Two

Eight 415th TFS and six 416th TFS F-117As attacked chemical and biological warfare facilities, the Republican Guard barracks, one missile facility, an airfield, ammunition stores, Central Intelligence Headquarters, Security Service Headquarters, and several highway bridges.

January 29   **Day 13, Wave Three**

The 415th TFS and the 416th TFS repeated the pattern of the first wave by flying four and six sorties, respectively. Objectives included the Rasheed Airfield, chemical and biological warfare facilities, the Republican Guard Headquarters in Baghdad, and ammunition bunkers, where 15 hits were recorded.

37th TFW (P) photo

37th TFW (P) photo

ABOVE LEFT:
A four-ship prepares to launch at Khamis Mushait Air Base.

ABOVE RIGHT:
"Sneak Attack," aircraft #821, loaded with GBU-27 and GBU-10 laser-guided bombs.

Day 14, Wave One
The 415th TFS attacked enemy targets with 10 F-117As. Most of the primary targets were obscured by poor weather. Pilots struck alternate targets, including highway bridges and an ammunition depot.

Day 14, Wave Two
Roughly 30 minutes after the first wave was launched, the 416th TFS launched the second wave. The aircraft hit ammunition dumps, the Presidential grounds, Iraqi Air Force Headquarters, Intelligence Service Headquarters, and a nuclear research center in Baghdad.

January 30   **Day 14, Wave Three**
The squadrons combined forces on the last wave of the day to bomb bridges. The 416th TFS was hampered by poor weather over the targets.

Day 15, Wave One
The squadrons again combined operations for the first combat wave of the night. Four 415th TFS aircraft joined six 416th TFS aircraft to attack bridges at Al Basrah, as well

37th TFW (P) photo

Maj. Joe Salata's "Midnight Reaper," #839 of the 415th TFS, reflecting 31 of its eventual 39 combat sorties.

37th TFW (P) photo

Capt. Rich Cline and maintenance crew pose in front of "It's Hammertime," aircraft #842 of the 416th TFS, which had 33 combat sorties at war's end.

as telephone exchanges, sector operations centers, and various other communication facilities. Despite bad weather pilots managed nine bomb hits.

January 30   **Day 15, Wave Two**

Just before midnight, 14 F-117As attacked bridges, airfield facilities, and communications systems.

January 31   **Day 15, Wave Three**

Seven jets attacked ammunition stores, as well as chemical and biological facilities. Eleven hits were recorded.

                      Day 16, Wave One

Nine F-117As from the 415th TFS and seven from the 416th TFS attacked bridges, communications systems, and ammunition stores. Twenty-three hits were recorded.

February 1   **Day 16, Wave Two**

Combined operations concentrated on bridges at Al Basrah, communications facilities, chemical bunkers, ammunition storage facilities, and Ubaydah Bin Al Jarrah Airfield.

Approximately 1,300 combat missions were flown by F-117A stealth pilots with over 2,000 tons of laser-guided munitions dropped on enemy targets.

Lt. Gen. Charles A. Horner, commander of Central Command Air Forces during Desert Storm, *stated: "Desert Storm was our first large-scale employment of the F-117A in combat. Their performance was eye-watering. The F-117 allowed us to do things that we could have only dreamed about in past conflicts. Stealth enabled us to gain surprise each and every day of the war."*

OPPOSITE PAGE, LOWER LEFT:
Crew chiefs in front of a fully loaded #818 "The Overachiever." Maintenance and support personnel worked around the clock ensuring extremely high readiness rates.

Day 17, Wave One
The first wave consisted of six aircraft from the 415th TFS and four from the 416th TFS. Nearly 2 1/2 hours into the mission the stealth fighters reached their objectives, hitting bridges and communications installations. In this strike, stealth pilots achieved 18 hits.

Day 17, Wave Two
The second wave concentrated on communications installations and military headquarters buildings, as well as airfields at Ahmed Al Jaber and Tallil. Six 415th TFS and seven 416th TFS aircraft joined in the attacks, scoring 20 hits.

February 2   **Day 17, Wave Three**
Five F-117As (three 415th TFS and two 416th TFS) attacked Tallil Airfield and ammunition storage facilities, scoring five hits.

Day 18, Wave One
Poor weather resulted in only two launches against an ammunition storage depot at Karbala, which was successfully attacked.

Day 18, Wave Two
The 415th TFS and 416th TFS launched a combined attack (six aircraft from each squadron) against hardened aircraft shelters at Ubaydah Bin Al Jarrah Airfield. Eleven hits were recorded.

February 3   **Day 19, Wave One**
Each squadron launched eight aircraft against Baghdad telephone exchanges, highway bridges, and the nuclear research center, as well as airfields and chemical/biological warfare facilities. Bad weather limited attack results to 17 hits—mostly on secondary targets.

February 4   **Day 19, Wave Two**
Twelve aircraft in mixed-unit operations attacked chemical warfare bunkers, bridges, and alternate airfield targets.

Day 20, Wave One
The first wave of four 415th TFS and five 416th TFS jets left before sunset to bomb Iraqi communications sites (primarily radio and television), where 14 bomb hits were recorded.

Day 20, Wave Two
The two squadrons combined forces for strikes against chemical warfare bunkers. Additional targets included the Ministry of Defense, Air Force, and Intelligence Service headquarters in Baghdad.

February 5   **Day 20, Wave Three**
Five 415th TFS and four 416th TFS aircraft joined in a concentrated attack against the chemical and biological warfare research laboratories at Salmon Pak. Independent operations by the 416th TFS targeted the short-range ballistic missile assembly plant in Baghdad, as well as other high-value targets in the area, including the Iraqi Air Force Headquarters.

Day 21, Wave One
Six 415th TFS and four 416th TFS jets attacked various missile production and launch facilities. Wing aircraft released 17 bombs and scored 17 direct hits.

Day 21, Wave Two
Twelve stealth fighters (six from each squadron) attacked hardened aircraft shelters on Balad Airfield. Also attacked were telecommunications centers, biological warfare facilities, ammunition depots, and headquarters buildings for the Iraqi Intelligence Service, Security Service, and the Republican Guard.

37th TFW (P) photo

February 6   Day 21, Wave Three
Twelve F-117As (six from each squadron) attacked chemical and biological warfare targets and ammunition depots. Pilots racked up 16 hits.

Day 22, Wave One
Hardened aircraft shelters, ammunition stores, fuel tanks, and the main runway at Rasheed Airfield were attacked by six 416th TFS pilots and four 415th TFS pilots, resulting in 15 direct hits in spite of poor weather.

Day 22, Wave Two
The wing sent 14 jets (eight from the 415th TFS and six from the 416th TFS) to attack chemical warfare sites and key targets in Baghdad, hitting 26 of their 27 targets.

February 7   Day 22, Wave Three
Ten sorties (four 415th TFS and six 416th TFS) attacked the Baghdad nuclear reactor, an airfield, a biological warfare facility, and an ammunition storage depot.

The accommodations at Khamis Mushait Air Base were first class. An F-117A maneuvers into one of the hardened aircraft facilities.

"The Toxic Avenger" taxis between hardened aircraft shelters at Khamis Mushait Air Base. Note the open drag chute doors between and just ahead of the vertical tail surfaces.

37th TFW (P) photo

37th TFW (P) photo

37th TFW (P) photo

A pair of F-117As taxi back to their hardened aircraft shelters following a predawn mission.

BELOW LEFT:
As a four-ship prepares to launch, another F-117A lifts off on its way to bomb Iraq.

BELOW RIGHT:
"Midnight Reaper," aircraft # 839 of the 415th TFS, flew 39 combat sorties during **Desert Storm.**

Day 23, Wave One
Twelve jets (six from each squadron) attacked communications sites, the Balad Air Defense Operations Center, key bunkers in Baghdad, and communications centers, scoring 18 direct hits.

Day 23, Wave Two
Another 12 F-117As (again, six from each squadron) converged on the chemical warfare facilities at Samarra, where pilots dropped 22 bombs with excellent results: only three missed their mark.

Wave Two, Milestone Event
A 416th TFS pilot, Capt. Scott Stimpert, achieved a milestone for the 37th TFW(P) as he delivered the 1000th F-117A bomb against Iraq in Operation *Desert Storm*. Stimpert's mission was against Samarra chemical warfare weapons bunkers, where he successfully dropped two bombs.

February 8   Day 23, Wave Three
Ten jets attacked chemical warfare bunkers, K-2 Airfield, a pumping station, a signals

37th TFW (P) photo

37th TFW (P) photo

BELOW:
Ordnance technicians make final adjustments to a GBU-10 laser-guided bomb.

UPPER RIGHT:
The thankless job of providing security 24 hours a day—every day. U.S. Air Force security police guarded against infiltrators and terrorists.

LOWER RIGHT:
Parked inside a hardened aircraft shelter at Khamis Mushait are two F-117As.

intelligence facility, and a radio relay station. Target evaluations revealed tremendous success—18 hits in 18 attempts.

Day 24, Wave One
Six aircraft from each squadron attacked various bunkers, where 20 bombs hit their targets.

Day 24, Wave Two
Twelve F-117As targeted the Rasheed and Al Taqaddam airfields, a liquid fuel rocket facility, a motor production plant, and a chemical warfare production factory.

February 9   **Day 24, Wave Three**

Ten sorties (four from the 415th TFS and six from the 416th TFS) were targeted against chemical warfare bunkers. Sixteen targets were struck.

37th TFW (P) photo

37th TFW (P) photo

37th TFW (P) photo

79

37th TFW (P) photo

Lt. Col. Greg Gonyea (right) and his crew chief in front of "Magic Hammer," aircraft #838 of the 416th TFS, which finished the war with 36 combat missions.

Much of the success enjoyed by the F-117As was due to the highly motivated and well-trained maintenance technicians of the 37th TFW(P).

37th TFW (P) photo

OPPOSITE PAGE:
Maj. Jeff Treadway exits his aircraft after shutting down the engines inside the hardened shelter at Khamis Mushait Air Base.

Day 25, Wave One

Targets for this wave included chemical warfare production facilities, an aircraft engine repair and test factory, bridges, and communications sites.

Day 25, Wave Two

Fourteen aircraft (six from the 415th TFS and eight from the 416th TFS) concentrated on various surface-to-air missile sites, communications centers, and key military targets in Baghdad, achieving 24 hits in as many attempts.

February 10   **Day 25, Wave Three**

The last wave included 10 aircraft targeted against ammunition depots and the Qayyarah West Airfield. Weather was a factor as only six hits were recorded.

Secretary of Defense Richard B. Cheney and Gen. Colin Powell, Chairman of the Joint Chiefs of Staff, visited the 37th TFW(P). Cheney commended the wing for doing a great job and for exceeding all expectations.

Day 26, Wave One

The 415th TFS launched four aircraft and the 416th TFS launched six to bomb Iraqi surface-to-air missile sites, where 18 hits were recorded.

37th TFW (P) photo

U.S. Air Force photo

U.S. Air Force photo

LEFT:
The F-117A was the only allied aircraft routinely assigned to targets in Baghdad. After months of training in the desert, stealth pilots scored impressive results once the war began.

37th TFW (P) photo

Capt. John Savidge (center), crew chiefs, and "Final Verdict," aircraft #814, which recorded 34 combat missions.

Maj. Jerry Sink and his crew chief pose with "Black Widow," aircraft #840, which flew 32 combat missions.

37th TFW (P) photo

February 11   **Day 26, Wave Two**

The second wave of eight aircraft were targeted against an armored vehicle repair facility, Saddam International Airfield buildings, and a liquid propellant plant. Six 416th TFS aircraft attacked hardened shelters, surface-to-surface missile production facilities, and a radio relay station.

Day 26, Wave Three

Ten aircraft (four from the 415th TFS and six from the 416th TFS) focused their attacks on Iraqi communications centers. Bombs were also dropped on a commando camp at Al Jahrah.

Day 27, Wave One

The 415th TFS led off with six aircraft, while the 416th TFS followed in takeoff sequence with four jets. Their targets included airfield and ammunition stores. Seventeen hits were recorded.

Day 27, Wave Two

The 416th TFS dispatched nine aircraft to bomb hardened aircraft shelters. Additional bombing raids struck the Iraqi Intelligence Services, the Ministry of Information, and the Ba'ath Party Headquarters. The 415th TFS sent six jets to attack hardened aircraft shelters. Pilots registered 23 hits.

February 12   ### Day 27, Wave Three

Ten jets in a mixed-unit operation bombed hardened aircraft shelters at several different airfields, as well as key targets in Baghdad, resulting in 17 direct hits.

Day 28, Wave One

The 415th TFS attacked the Ministry of Defense building in Baghdad, as well as numerous other targets, scoring 15 direct hits.

Day 28, Wave Two

Eight 415th TFS and six 416th TFS jets bombed a fighter direction post/interceptor operations center, various radio and television communications centers, and the Iraqi Central Intelligence Agency in Baghdad. The Ba'ath Party building was also revisited. Twenty-two hits were recorded.

February 13   ### Day 28, Wave Three

Four 415th TFS and six 416th TFS aircraft were launched to bomb bridges; missile sites; command, control and communications bunkers; and various headquarters buildings in Baghdad. Pilots recorded 17 hits.

Day 29, Wave One

Six 415th TFS and four 416th TFS jets attacked a military barracks, as well as communications facilities, command posts, and a commando camp, achieving 15 direct hits.

February 14   ### Day 29, Wave Two

Fourteen jets (six from the 415th TFS and eight from the 416th TFS) attacked Iraqi military barracks and garrisons at Al Abrad, communications sites, and airfield bunkers at Kirkuk.

Day 29, Wave Three

The final wave of attacks for the night concentrated on communications sites in Baghdad, radar sites, and the Navy Headquarters at Al Basrah.

Day 30, Wave One

Ten F-117As attacked hardened aircraft shelters, along with surface-to-air missile sites and a rocket motor test facility. Pilots struck successfully with 15 hits.

Day 30, Wave Two

The wing launched 14 aircraft against a nuclear weapons facility, ammunition depots, command posts, and communications sites at Al Basrah. Pilots scored 22 direct hits.

February 15   ### Day 30, Wave Three

Four 415th TFS jets bombed communications sites, while six 416th TFS aircraft attacked an assortment of targets—including military garrisons, a radar facility, and communications sites—recording 16 hits.

DoD photo

37th TFW (P) photo

OPPOSITE PAGE
LOWER LEFT AND RIGHT:
Throughout the war, F-117As successfully attacked hard-to-hit bridges in an effort to cut off Iraqi resupply activities. From the opening hours of the war, high priority was given to the Iraqi early warning communications network. Once these targets were neutralized, non-stealth air assets were given greater flexibility (and survivability) in pressing attacks to their assigned targets.

THIS PAGE:
Very few enemy targets were safe from the laser-guided GBU-10 and GBU-27 munitions dropped by the F-117As and many other aircraft of the coalition air forces. The use of the laser-guided bombs on hardened aircraft shelters rendered much of the Iraqi Air Force inoperable.

Day 31, Wave One

Six 415th TFS aircraft went after Baghdad's aircraft repair depot, a chemical/biological facility, a Scud missile production facility, and two surface-to-air sites. The 416th TFS launched four aircraft to attack five missile sites, a chemical/biological research plant, and a missile production site. F-117A pilots achieved 16 direct hits.

Day 31, Wave Two

In preparation for the start of the ground war, the second wave was tasked with the destruction of elements of Iraq's extensive barrier system. Six F-117As of the 415th TFS and eight from the 416th TFS attacked distribution points and pump stations. Stealth pilots also attacked a missile research and development facility. Pilots scored 24 hits, including the destruction of the T-junctions, distribution points, and pump stations.

February 16   **Day 31, Wave Three**

The 415th TFS attacked a missile research and development facility and a missile production plant. Two jets went after a suspected missile facility and a rocket engine test facility. The 416th TFS concentrated on similar targets with, by now, routine precision—14 direct hits.

Day 32, Wave One

Rather than three waves with intermixed squadron forces, the wing set up a wave of 14 jets from each unit. The 416th TFS conducted strikes against hardened aircraft shelters at three airfields, as well as the railroad yard at Al Basrah. In all, 21 targets were successfully attacked.

DoD photo

DoD photo

Day 32, Wave Two

Two hours after the first wave, the 415th TFS launched its 14 jets. Four aircraft revisited the Al Basrah rail yard, while others attacked tactical direction sites; radio transmitters, receivers, and relays; a repeater station; military barracks; and missile support facilities. This wave delivered 24 direct hits.

February 17   **Day 33, Wave One**

Thirty-four combat missions were scheduled against targets in Iraq. Ten pilots attacked ammunition depots, surface-to-air missile sites, chemical/biological warfare research facilities, and the new airfield at Wadi Al Khirr.

Day 33, Wave Two

The second wave attacked chemical/biological warfare research facilities, an arms plant, the Wadi Al Khirr Airfield, surface-to-surface missile storage plants, a Scud assembly factory, a motor case production plant, and an artillery production plant. Twenty-three targets were demolished.

February 18   **Day 33, Wave Three**

The final sorties of the night were flown against two Scud plants and a solid propellant assembly plant, where nine pilots scored 14 direct hits.

Maj. Bob Eskridge gives the ever-present "thumbs up" prior to another combat sortie.

37th TFW (P) photo

37th TFW (P) photo

Capt. Dennis Baker and his crew chief, like all other F-117A pilots and crew chiefs, worked closely throughout the war, achieving a mission-ready rate higher than ever before experienced in peacetime.

Day 34, Wave One

Pilots of the two squadrons set out at dusk to destroy nuclear research facilities in Baghdad. Weather obscured the primary targets. Pilots attacked back-up targets, with eight direct hits on a road bridge and an ammunition storage facility. The 416th TFS had better luck with the weather, allowing them to deliver nine bombs on target. Another 416th TFS aircraft added two more direct hits in an attack on a previously targeted ammunition storage facility.

February 18   **Day 34, Wave Two**

Stealth pilots attacked hangars at Baghdad Muthenna Airfield, an ammunition dump, and the new Iraqi Air Force Headquarters in Baghdad. Fourteen aircraft in a mixed-unit operation achieved an impressive hit ratio by putting 26 of 28 bombs on target.

February 19   **Day 34, Wave Three**

The third wave attacked an airfield and a tunnel.

Day 35, Wave One

The night's first wave concentrated on three familiar targets in Iraq: Baghdad's nuclear research facilities, Karbala's ammunition storage facility, and Latifiya's solid propellant plant. Two aircraft also bombed a suspected biological warfare facility. Stealth pilots scored 28 direct hits.

February 20   **Day 35, Wave Two**

Jalibah Southeast Airfield was the sole target for 10 F-117As. Bad weather hampered all 10 sorties and no bombs were dropped.

Day 36, Wave One

Four 415th TFS and six 416th TFS aircraft attacked strategic railroad bridges and a chemical plant. Four 415th TFS aircraft put eight bombs directly on target at the chemical plant. The 416th TFS put nine bombs on target.

February 21   **Day 36, Wave Two**

Targets included ammunition storage facilities, an arms plant, a rocket motor plant, an ammunition depot, and the Al Taqaddum Airfield. Pilots of the 415th TFS achieved a 12-for-12 bombing score. The 416th TFS's pilots took on the balance of the night's work, putting 14 bombs on target.

Day 37, Wave One

Radio relays, bridges, bunkers, and an early warning facility were among the targets attacked by six 415th TFS pilots. Nine bombs found their mark. Meanwhile, four 416th TFS jets targeted an international radio communications transmitter in Baghdad and chemical production facilities, and scored eight hits for eight attempts.

Day 37, Wave Two

Fourteen F-117As attacked suspected biological weapons storage and production facilities, a fiber optics repeater station, a radio relay station, and the H-2 Airfield. The 415th TFS scored 11 hits, while the 416th scored 13 hits.

February 22   Day 37, Wave Three

Targets included a railroad yard, radio communications equipment, highway bridges, ammunition storage bunkers, an underground nuclear facility, and a Scud missile plant.

Day 38, Wave One

Ten aircraft (four 415th TFS and six 416th TFS) attacked targets in Baghdad, a Scud missile production facility, and a steel fabrication plant. The research facility in Baghdad received 10 hits from four 415th TFS pilots and one 416th TFS pilot. Remaining 416th pilots added seven hits on other targets.

Day 38, Wave Two

Eight F-117As of the 415th TFS and six 416th TFS jets attacked a nuclear research facility in Baghdad, where pilots pounded the target with 19 direct hits.

February 23   Day 38, Wave Three

Ten jets (four from the 415th TFS and six from the 416th TFS) attacked the Iraqi Intelligence and Special Operations headquarters. Stealth pilots scored 15 direct hits.

Day 39, Wave One

Just before sunset, in preparation for the ground offensive, 31 F-117As were launched within 44 minutes. The largest stealth fighter attack to date concentrated attacks on a bomb assembly plant and headquarters buildings in Baghdad, a chemical warfare site, a possible nuclear facility, and an arms plant. Forty-four bombs landed squarely on target.

February 24   Day 39, Wave Two

Four jets from the 415th TFS and two from the 416th TFS attacked communications equipment and facilities. Bad weather over the target limited bombing activity so only four bombs were dropped.

Day 40, Wave One

Four 415th TFS and six 416th TFS aircraft attacked a possible fuze plant, a chemical storage building, and another target. Nineteen bombs hit their targets.

Day 40, Wave Two

Fourteen jets were launched to revisit the fuze factory, the special security services facility in Baghdad, and an ammunition dump, as well as another high-priority target. Eighteen direct hits were recorded.

February 25   Day 40, Wave Three

The 415th TFS launched four fighters with six 416th TFS jets to strike targets in and around Baghdad. Bad weather prohibited bomb release over Baghdad, but alternate targets suffered when 11 out of 12 bombs scored hits.

February 26   Day 41

CENTAF cancelled all stealth missions due to poor weather.

Day 42, Wave One

The wing initiated a 32-turn-32 flying schedule with each squadron contributing 16 aircraft. The 416th launched aircraft only to encounter poor weather over Iraq. Most aircraft returned without having dropped their bombs.

February 27   Day 42, Wave Two

Poor weather continued to inhibit stealth fighter operations. Of the 27 sorties launched, only eight bombs were dropped, but with effective results as all eight were direct hits.

Day 43, Wave One

Back on track, Team Stealth launched 10 aircraft from each squadron and enjoyed a bomb score of 32 for 32 as they devastated the Ba'ath Party Headquarters and the Muthenna Airfield in Baghdad, as well as a chemical/biological research facility.

Day 43, Wave Two

Five aircraft from each squadron attacked a missile research, development, and production plant and a rocket motor test facility.

At 11:30 p.m., Headquarters Air Forces canceled the night's third wave. The commander of the 37th TFW(P) was instructed to put future attacks against Iraqi targets on hold—but to stand by in case events dictated renewed assaults.

February 28   Air Campaign Ends

At 12:15 a.m., CENTAF relayed the good news that all operations were suspended in order to give the Iraqis an opportunity to sign a cease-fire agreement.

Pilots wave to a homecoming crowd of 25,000 at Nellis AFB, NV, following the wing's redeployment stateside, April 1, 1991.

U.S. Air Force photo

Randy Jolly is a freelance photographer specializing in military aviation and defense images. His photos have appeared in many books and on the covers of *Newsweek, Aviation Week,* and numerous other defense magazines throughout the world. He is the author of *The Real Heroes*, a large format picture book on the U.S. Air Force, also published by Specialty Press. Mr. Jolly lives in Dallas, Texas, with his wife and two children. He is the president of AeroGraphics.

Robert Shelton, Jr., is an 18-year veteran of military service. As chief of public affairs for the initial Stealth unit, he became an integral part of the F-117A story. In fact, he is the Air Force's only public affairs technician to have been selected to work directly with an operational F-117A unit. In 1990, he spent eight-and-a-half months in Saudi Arabia as chief of public affairs for the 37th Tactical Fighter Wing (the only Stealth unit to serve in Operations *Desert Shield* and *Desert Storm*). Mr. Shelton lives in Las Vegas, Nevada, with his wife and two daughters. He is now chief of media relations at Nellis Air Force Base.